Church Basics

Understanding
Church Leadership

Series Editor Jonathan Leeman
Author Mark Dever

B&H
PUBLISHING GROUP
Nashville, Tennessee

978-1-4336-8892-8

Published by B&H Publishing Group
Nashville, Tennessee

Dewey Decimal Classification: 262
Subject Heading: LEADERSHIP \ CHURCH POLITY \
CHURCH WORK

3 4 5 6 7 8 9 10 • 21 20 19 18 17

CONTENTS

CHURCH BASICS SERIES PREFACE

The Christian life is the churched life. This basic biblical conviction informs every book in the Church Basics series.

That conviction in turn affects how each author treats his topic. For instance, *Understanding the Lord's Supper* maintains that the Lord's Supper is not a private, mystical act between you and Jesus. It is a meal around the family table in which you commune with Christ and Christ's people. *Understanding the Great Commission* contends that the Great Commission is not a license to head into the nations as Jesus' witness all by oneself. It is a charge given to the whole church to be fulfilled by the whole church. *Understanding the Congregation's Authority* observes that the authority of the church rests not only with the leaders, but with the entire assembly. Every member has a job to do, including you.

Every book is written *for* the average church member, and this is a crucial point. If the Christian life is a churched life, then you, a baptized believer and church member, have a responsibility to understand these basic topics. Just as Jesus charges you with promoting and protecting his gospel message, so he charges you with promoting and protecting his gospel people, the church. These books will explain how.

You are like a shareholder in Christ's gospel ministry corporation. And what do good shareholders do? They study their company, study the market, and study the competition. They want the most out of their investment. You, Christian, have invested your whole life in the gospel. The purpose of the series, then, is to help you maximize the health and kingdom profitability of your local congregation for God's glorious gospel ends.

Are you ready to get to work?

Jonathan Leeman
Series Editor

Books in the Church Basics series

Understanding the Great Commission, Mark Dever
Understanding Baptism, Bobby Jamieson
Understanding the Lord's Supper, Bobby Jamieson
Understanding the Congregation's Authority, Jonathan Leeman
Understanding Church Discipline, Jonathan Leeman
Understanding Church Leadership, Mark Dever

For further instruction on these topics from these authors (B&H):

Don't Fire Your Church Members: The Case for Congregationalism, Jonathan Leeman

Going Public: Why Baptism Is Required for Church Membership, Bobby Jamieson

Baptist Foundations: Church Government for an Anti-Institutional Age, Mark Dever and Jonathan Leeman, editors

Preach: Theology Meets Practice, Mark Dever and Greg Gilbert
The Church: The Gospel Made Visible, Mark Dever

Introduction

The issue of leadership in the local church is a crucial topic.

Consider, after all, Christ's love for the church. He gave himself for the church. He identifies with it as his own body. He continues to care and provide for it through his Word, Spirit, and ministers. And he promises to reveal the church on the last day as his resplendent bride. If all this is true, those who lead the church have a high and holy responsibility. Think of how care-*full* a bride's attendants are as they prepare her to walk down the aisle.

Christ wants his leaders no less careful as they prepare his bride. For this reason it is worth spending time in studying, reflecting on, and praying through what God's Word says about church leadership.

The Next Big Thing

To be sure, church leadership can be a divisive issue. You can well imagine the kind of reactions a young pastor in an old church gets when he recommends changing the leadership structures. A few years ago, retired pastor of First Baptist Houston John Bisagno observed that the topic of church government is one of the most divisive issues in Baptist churches today.

Part of the problem is that every few years pastors' conferences and publishers get everyone excited about *the next big thing*. And often the next big thing comes from the corporate world. Here is one pastor—from the 1950s—describing his own leadership structure. Is he describing a church or a bank?

> The first step I undertook when I became pastor of Druid
> Hills Church was to set up the Pastor's Cabinet, composed of
> the heads of all the departments of the church life—Chairman
> and Vice-Chairman of the Board of Deacons, Chairman and
> Vice-Chairman of the Finance Committee, Chairman of the
> Trustees, Chairman of the Board of Ushers, Clerk, Treasurer,
> Chairman of the Relief Committee, Superintendent of the
> Sunday School, Director of the Training Union, President of
> the Woman's Missionary Society, President of the Brotherhood,
> Minister of Music, Chairman of the Music Committee,
> Chairman of the Guest Book Committee, Chairman of the
> Youth Council, Librarian, and Members of the Church Staff.[1]

What confidence we can have in our corporate organizational structures!

Would the Christians of earlier eras have approved of the plethora of non-biblical offices in our churches? Well, they certainly recognized that some matters of leadership and governance must be left to prudence. The 1742 Philadelphia Baptist Confession observes that the Scriptures "expressly set down" everything necessary for faith and life, which includes how churches should be organized. But then the confession goes on to acknowledge that "there are some circumstances concerning the worship of God, and government of the church, common to human actions and societies; which are to be ordered by the light of nature, and Christian prudence, according to the general rules of the word, which are always to be observed." In other words, church government is a matter in which some latitude is appropriate. Christians have always acknowledged this.

At the same time, Christians have also recognized that Scripture contains specific instructions about the local church's polity. And before we spend lots of time thinking about ways that leadership changes between one context and another, we should begin by considering what the Bible says for everyone.

Purpose of This Book

What model of leadership does the Bible recommend?

Several years ago I was asked to contribute to a "multiple-views" book on the topic of church government. The purpose of the "multiple-views" book is to ask representatives of different traditions to present their viewpoints. They can be useful, but I declined. The difficulty was, the editor asked if I would offer either the "senior pastor" view, or the "congregational" view, or the "plurality of elders" view. In fact, I believe that Scripture commends all of these! Congregations benefit from having a senior or lead pastor *and* a plurality of elders lead *in the context* of congregationalism. We need a happy helping of each, coexisting and reinforcing each other in the life of the local church.

In his book *Understanding the Congregation's Authority,* which belongs to the same series as this one, Jonathan Leeman spends most of his time discussing congregational authority. But he concludes by placing the discussion into the context of plural elder leadership. In this book, I will do the opposite. I will spend most of my time discussing plural elder leadership (together with diaconal service), but will conclude by placing this conversation into the context of congregationalism. Who are the deacons and elders? What do they do? How do they relate to one another, and how do elders relate to the congregation as a whole? In case you have read my earlier book *A Display of God's Glory,* you will find much of that material here, albeit reshaped around the topic of leadership.

Speaking personally as a Baptist pastor for a moment, I have found having a plurality of elders immensely helpful in equipping the members of the congregation to fulfill their congregational authority and responsibility. Why have one teacher and shepherd when you could have a number of them? More gifts! More equipping getting done! More saints being built up to do the work of the ministry!

Our church's contributions to our Baptist denomination (the Southern Baptist Convention) have not fallen; they have increased. My pastoral leadership has not been compromised by serving with these other men; it has been enhanced. We have never once been tempted to baptize infants! And our congregation has not become more passive in ministry, but more active. Each elder is a gift of Christ to his church.

On the Gift of Authority

Of course, it is not always easy to view those in authority as a gift. Ever since the Fall, authority has often been abused, and it is healthy to acknowledge as much. Power apart from God's purposes is always demonic.

At the same time, it is not good to suspect all authority. If we are to live as God means us to live, we must be able to trust him, and this includes trusting the ones made in his image whom he has placed in positions of authority. Everyone in the Bible from Adam and Eve to the rogue rulers in the book of Revelation show their evil fundamentally by denying God's authority, and usurping it as their own.

It is a great privilege to be served by godly leaders. And godly leadership is a gift. To reject authority, as so many in our day do, is short-sighted and self-destructive. A world without authority would be like desires with no restraints, a car with no controls, an intersection with no traffic lights, a game with no rules, a home with no parents, a world without God. It could go on for a little while, but before long it would seem pointless, then cruel, and finally tragic.

Despite our tendency to ignore it, godly and biblical leadership is crucial to building a church that glorifies God. Our exercise of leadership in the church relates to God's nature and character. When we exercise proper authority through the law, around the family table, in our jobs, in the Scout troop, in our homes, and especially in the church, we help to display God's image to creation. This is the call on a church's leaders. What a privilege it is to lead, and what a privilege it is to support their work!

CHAPTER 1

Who Are the Deacons?

Let's begin with one of the most familiar offices in many churches today—the office of deacon. Depending on what kind of church you come from, "deacon" may conjure up images of gray-haired bankers sitting around long, highly-varnished tables in opulently appointed church parlors. Or maybe the word brings to mind earnest servants of the church coordinating needs-based ministries, evangelistic outreach, or pastoral care.

Who does the Bible say deacons are?

"Deacon" Defined

In our modern translations of the New Testament, the Greek word *diakonos* is usually translated as "servant" and sometimes as "minister." Sometimes it is just transliterated as "deacon." It can refer to service in general,[2] to rulers in particular,[3] or to caring for physical needs.[4] It is clear in the New Testament that women can do at least some of this serving.[5] Angels serve in this way.[6] It sometimes refers to waiting tables.[7]

The New Testament world was similar to our own in the way it viewed servanthood. Service to others was not admired by the Greeks. Instead, they admired developing one's own character and personality always with an eye to maintaining self-respect. Diaconal service to others would have been regarded pejoratively as "servile."

The Bible and Jesus, though, present service quite differently. If we were to transliterate (and not translate) the key words in John 12:26, we would hear Jesus saying, "If anyone *deacons* Me, he must follow Me. Where I am, there My *deacon* also will be. If anyone *deacons* me, the Father will honor him." In Matthew 20:26, we would hear him saying, "Whoever wants to be great, must be your *deacon*." And in Matthew 23:11: "The greatest among you will be your *deacon*."

In fact, Jesus presented himself as a type of deacon.[8] And the Bible presents Christians as deacons of Christ or his gospel. So the apostles are depicted as deacons, and Paul regularly refers to himself and to those who worked with him as deacons.[9] He refers to himself as a deacon among the Gentiles.[10] Paul calls Timothy a deacon of Christ,[11] and Peter says that the Old Testament prophets were deacons to us Christians.[12] The Bible also calls angels deacons. Satan, too, has his deacons.[13]

We should always be careful to maintain a distinction between the ministry of deacons and the ministry of elders. In one sense both elders and deacons are involved in "deaconing," but that service takes on two very different forms, both of which we see in Acts 6. There the apostles say that they should not "serve tables" because they are responsible for the "ministry of the word" (vv. 2–4 ESV). The words translated as "serve" and "ministry" are different forms of the same Greek root. Can you guess what it is? *Deacon!* So you have traditional deaconing (table-waiting, physical service), and you have the kind of "deaconing" of the Word to which God called the apostles (and later, elders).

We will look at this passage more in the next chapter. But the men described in Acts 6 are very much like the church's waiters, at least in an administrative sense. They are to care for the physical needs of the church. And a church needs both types of deaconing—of the Word (elders) and of tables (deacons)—so that one is not confused with the other and neither is forgotten. Churches should neglect neither the preaching of the Word nor the practical care for the members that helps to foster unity. Both of these aspects of a church's life and ministry are important. In order to ensure that both kinds of deaconing occur in our churches, we should distinguish the ministry of the deacons from the ministry of the elders.

Qualifications of Deacons

Drawing from Acts 6, we can say that those who serve as deacons should be known to be "full of the Spirit and wisdom" (v. 3). They might be concerned with physical things, but theirs is a spiritual ministry. Such spiritual-minded wisdom enables them to oversee church resources in a manner that serves the unity of the flock. They should be chosen by the congregation and possess the congregation's confidence. And they should willingly and diligently take on the responsibility for the particular needs of their ministry.

In 1 Timothy 3:8–13, Paul spells out further what deacons should be like. They should be worthy of respect, sincere, not indulging in much wine, not pursuing dishonest gain, keeping hold of the deep truths of the faith with a clear conscience, tested and approved servants who are the husband of but one wife, and able managers of their children and household.

The command to be the "husband of one wife" does not preclude women from serving in diaconal positions. The example of Phoebe the "deacon" in Romans 16:1 (NIV), the use of "deacon" words elsewhere of women in the Scriptures, and to a lesser degree, the long history of deaconesses in Baptist churches has led my own church to embrace the ministry of women as deaconesses. That said, 1 Timothy 2 prohibits women from serving as elders. So if a church confuses the role of elders and deacons (as in many Baptist churches today), we would discourage it from recognizing women as deacons. We can freely encourage our sisters to be recognized as deaconesses when the distinction between the offices of elder and deacon is clear.

Historical Background

Scholars disagree about how fluid the structures of the churches were in the first few decades after Pentecost. But pretty early churches possessed a plurality of elders and a plurality of deacons. Think of how Paul greets the church in Philippi: "To all the saints in Christ Jesus who are in Philippi, including the overseers [or elders] and deacons" (Phil. 1:1).

Immediately after New Testament times, these separate offices of elders and deacons continued. The role of elders began to be distinguished between bishops and priests, but deacons continued to be listed in early documents after the bishops and priests. Usually they were tasked with assisting the bishops or overseers. In the early church, the office generally seems to have been held for life. The functions of the office, however, varied from place to place.

Diaconal duties might include:

- reading or singing Scripture in church;
- receiving the offerings and keeping records of who gave;
- distributing the offerings to the bishops, presbyters, and themselves; to the unmarried women and widows; and to the poor;
- distributing communion;
- leading prayers during gatherings, and giving a signal for those who were not to take communion to leave before the ordinance was administered.

This summarizes the duties of deacons from the second through the sixth centuries.

As the monarchical episcopate developed, so did a kind of monarchical diaconate beneath it. As the role of bishop developed, so did the role of archdeacon. The archdeacon was the chief deacon of a particular place and might be described as a deputy concerned with material matters. Unsurprisingly, the archdeacon in Rome became particularly important. Abuses eventually crept into the office of deacon, and deacons—especially archdeacons—became quite wealthy. How ironic that those who were meant to serve others instead used others to serve their own desires!

For a number of reasons, the deacons' influence declined in the Middle Ages. Caring for the poor became more a vehicle for the contributors to gain credit with God in order to lessen their time in purgatory.

The Eastern Orthodox Church has always kept separate deacons—laymen who served in that capacity. In the West, though, by the late Middle Ages, being a deacon had become a step on the way to being ordained as a priest. Deacons in the Roman Catholic and the Episcopalian churches are still just that—trainee ministers who serve as deacons for one year before becoming full-fledged priests. However, the Second Vatican Council has reopened the possibility of a different, permanent, more biblical kind of deacon in the Roman Catholic Church.

Martin Luther recovered the church's responsibility to care physically for the church and especially for the poor in the church, though Lutheran churches didn't recover the idea of the New Testament deacon. In the Lutheran churches today, practice varies. In some places deacons are not ordained, but in other places any ordained assistant minister would be called a deacon, particularly those with responsibilities for pastoral care and evangelism.

In many of the more evangelical Protestant churches during the Reformation, the biblical practice of distinguishing deacons and elders or pastors grew. Some Protestants, like Martin Bucer at Cambridge, urged that the duties of the deacons should be reestablished. Deacons, these voices said, should work to distinguish between the deserving and the undeserving poor. They should discretely investigate and quietly care for the needs of the one while refusing the other. They should also keep written records, as they were able, of funds given by church members.

In Presbyterian churches, deacons administer the alms and care for the poor and sick (though recently we might argue that these functions have largely been taken over by the secular state). The deacons are a separate body from the elders and are responsible to them.

Many Baptist and congregational churches, too, once distinguished the two offices of elders and deacons, and more and more are recovering this biblical vision. But in some other churches, the elders' work is assigned to the deacons. They assist the pastor in various ways, especially in distributing the elements at the Lord's Supper, and they have evolved into a kind of executive and financial board for the church, particularly in congregations that no longer have boards of elders. Deacons often serve actively for limited periods of time, though their recognition as a "deacon" is usually considered permanent.

This is how some churches have done it. Do the Scriptures have any instructions for us by which to reform our practices?

CHAPTER 2

What Do Deacons Do?

As we have seen, the deacon's work appears many times in the New Testament. The clearest picture of a deacon's work, though, possibly comes from Acts 6.

> In those days, as the number of the disciples was multiplying, there arose a complaint by the Hellenistic Jews against the Hebraic Jews that their widows were being overlooked in the daily distribution. Then the Twelve summoned the whole company of the disciples and said, "It would not be right for us to give up preaching about God to handle [*deacon*] financial matters. Therefore, brothers, select from among you seven men of good reputation, full of the Spirit and wisdom, whom we can appoint to this duty. But we will devote ourselves to prayer and to the preaching ministry [*deacon*]." The proposal pleased the whole company. So they chose Stephen, a man full of faith and the Holy Spirit, and Philip, Prochorus, Nicanor, Timon, Parmenas, and Nicolaus, a proselyte from Antioch. They had them stand before the apostles, who prayed and laid their hands on them.
>
> So the preaching about God flourished, the number of the disciples in Jerusalem multiplied greatly, and a large group of priests became obedient to the faith. (vv. 1–7)

The office of deacon is not named, but the word *deacon* is used as a verb to describe what these seven individuals will do (translated as "handle" in verse 3). And even if the seven men appointed here are not official deacons, the passage helps us to see three aspects of a deacon's ministry.[14]

Care for the Physical Needs of the Church

First, deacons care for the physical needs of the church. Some of the widows were being overlooked in the daily distribution of food. I already said that the word *deacon* means minister or servant, and it was particularly used of table-waiters at the time, or other types of service, usually physical or financial. The apostles characterized this service as "handling financial matters" (HCSB) or "waiting on tables" (ESV)—literally "deaconing tables."

The deacons in Acts 6 probably didn't do all the deaconing themselves. Rather these few deacons probably organized and facilitated the work of other members in the church in making sure these widows were taken care of. After all, the Jerusalem church had thousands of members.

Caring for people, especially other members of our churches, is important for three reasons: 1) It serves their physical well-being; 2) it serves their spiritual well-being; 3) and it serves as a witness to the world outside. Remember Jesus' words: "By this all people will know that you are My disciples, if you have love for one another" (John 13:35). The physical care presented in Acts 6 demonstrates that Christlike love.

Work for Unity in the Body

Behind this first purpose for the people in need, though, we see in Acts 6 a larger purpose for the body as a whole: deacons work for the unity of the church body.

Consider again what these seven individuals were tasked with doing. They were to make the food distribution among the widows more equitable, yes. But why was that important? Because this physical neglect was causing spiritual disunity in the body. Notice the passage begins with the report of complaining about one group in the church against another. And this arrested the attention of the apostles. They were not merely resolving a benevolence ministry problem in the church. They wanted to stop the church's unity from fracturing, and in a particularly dangerous way: along traditional ethnic lines of division. The deacons were appointed to head off disunity in the church.

Really, this is the goal for all the gifts that God's Spirit gives to his church—to build one another up and encourage each other (e.g., Rom. 1:11–12). Paul tells the Corinthians that their gifts should be exercised "for the common good" (1 Cor. 12:4–7, 12 ESV). He again exhorts them, "Since you are eager for gifts of the spirit, try to excel in those that build up the church" (1 Cor. 14:12 NIV). A little later he adds, "all must be done for strengthening" (14:26, author's translation). John Calvin, commenting on chapter 14, suggested, "The more anxious a person is to devote himself to upbuilding, the more highly Paul wishes him to be regarded." Peter therefore commands, "Each should use whatever gift he has received to serve others administering God's grace" (1 Pet. 4:10, author paraphrase). Likewise, the ministry of the deacons in Acts 6 is to build up the body by working for unity.

Here's one application for our churches: You don't want people serving as deacons who are unhappy with your church. The deacons should never be the ones who complain the loudest or jar the church with their actions or attitudes. Quite the opposite! The deacons should be mufflers or shock absorbers.

Here's another application: You don't want turfy and small-minded people serving as deacons, or people who quietly resent interlopers in their sphere. You want people who care about the whole church, and not just their area of ministry and their prerogatives in that area. Yes, they address needs in their area, but they do so on behalf of the whole, and in a way that contributes to the health of the whole. They don't advocate for their cause like lobbyists who are unconcerned with what costs might be imposed on others. In fact, they help people working with them to see that work as part of uniting and edifying the whole.

Deacons help to bind the church together with cords of kindness and loving service. They are church builders.

Support the Ministry of the Word

Thirdly, the seven individuals appointed in Acts 6 worked to support the ministry of the Word. The apostles acknowledged that caring for physical needs was a responsibility of the whole church, and therefore, in some sense, their responsibility, too. But they turned this responsibility over to another group within the church so that they could attend to the ministry of the Word and prayer.

They were servants who served the church as a whole by helping with the responsibilities that the main teachers could not perform. And in so doing they supported and encouraged the teachers of the Word in their ministry.

Another application: you don't want to nominate deacons who don't recognize the importance of the ministry of preaching and teaching, but people who are anxious to protect it. More broadly, you want the most supportive people in the church to serve as the deacons. So when you're considering who might serve as a deacon, look for people with gifts of encouragement.

At my church in Washington, D.C., we recognize our deacons not as a deliberative body, but rather as those people who coordinate particular needed ministries in the church. Nowhere does the New Testament prescribe two deliberative bodies, and having them presents many practical difficulties. Instead, we have a deacon who supervises our ministry of hospitality; another who coordinates our ministry through the website; another who handles our sound system; another for parking, and so on. As of this writing, we have twenty-two different deacons serving us in diaconal positions. We regularly retire positions that no longer need coordination, or we split burgeoning ones into two or even three positions, as we did with the deacons of childcare and sound. When a new need or opportunity becomes apparent in the church, we create a new diaconal position to serve that need. See the appendix to get a sample of several deacon job descriptions used in my church.

We also hope that these deacons will be some of the leading utilizers of the church's human resources. One of their goals is to get to know the whole body so that they can work to coordinate others in pushing forward the ministry of the church as a whole. This service that they perform for us is costly. They must regard their deaconship as their main ministry in the church while they serve in that position. But what a blessing such servants are to the church as they work to develop hearts of service in other brothers and sisters! Through their activity and creativity, our deacons will bless our church for far longer than they hold the office.

In summary, the New Testament brings together the three aspects of deacon ministry that we've noted in Acts 6—care for physical needs to the end of uniting the body under the ministers of the Word. They should be encouragers, peacemakers, and servants. In my church, the elders nominate a man or a woman when a need is present and they find someone who exemplifies these virtues. The congregation then votes to affirm these nominations. As Dietrich Bonhoeffer said, "The church does not need brilliant personalities but faithful servants of Jesus and the brethren."[15]

CHAPTER 3

Who Are the Elders?

As important as the deacons are, even more fundamental to our life together as Christians in churches is the ministry of another group—the elders. In the New Testament, the words for elder, overseer, and pastor are used interchangeably, which means I will use them interchangeably as well (see Acts 20:17, 28; 1 Pet. 5:1–2; see also, Eph. 4:11).

Plurality of Elders

The first thing to note about the pastors or elders of a local church is that they are plural. The New Testament never mentions a specific number of elders for a congregation, but it regularly refers to "elders" in the plural:

- "When they had appointed *elders* in every church and prayed with fasting, they committed them to the Lord" (Acts 14:23; see also 11:30; 15:2, 4, 6, 22–23);
- "they delivered the decisions reached by the apostles and *elders* at Jerusalem for them to observe" (Acts 16:4);
- "he sent to Ephesus and called for the *elders* of the church" (Acts 20:17);
- "The following day Paul went in with us to James, and all the *elders* were present" (Acts 21:18);

- "Do not neglect the gift that is in you; it was given to you through prophecy, with the laying on of hands by the *council of elders*" (1 Tim. 4:14; see also 5:17);
- "The reason I left you in Crete was to set right what was left undone and, as I directed you, to appoint *elders* in every town" (Titus 1:5);
- "Is anyone among you sick? He should call for the *elders* of the church, and they should pray over him" (James 5:14);
- "I exhort the *elders* among you" (1 Pet. 5:1).

The pattern is nearly uniform and the evidence overwhelming. In fact, the only singular reference to an elder occurs in 2 and 3 John, where the writer simply refers to himself as "the elder," and in 1 Timothy 5, where Paul offers instruction for an accusation against "an elder." Essentially, the New Testament uniformly presents churches as led by a body of elders, not simply one elder.

Qualifications for Elders

Who should be an elder and what should the qualifications be? Paul tells us in 1 Timothy 2 and 3 and Titus 1.

Paul teaches in 1 Timothy 2:12, "I do not allow a woman to teach or to have authority over a man." Whatever the exact kind of authority Paul had in mind here, he did not want women teaching men in the church, which means reserving the office of elder for men. The early church, in other words, mirrored the creation order of the authority of the husband over the wife in the practice of the church.

What about Galatians 3:28, which wonderfully observes that there is neither male nor female in Christ? The point here is to affirm our equal worth and standing before God's throne as those who have been saved by grace alone. This is not meant to eliminate all distinctions between the genders any more than it eliminates men's and women's distinct roles in childbirth.

Paul then offers a fuller list of qualifications in 1 Timothy 3 (see also Titus 1:5–9):

> This saying is trustworthy: "If anyone aspires to be an overseer, he desires a noble work." An overseer, therefore, must be above reproach, the husband of one wife, self-controlled, sensible, respectable, hospitable, an able teacher, not addicted to wine, not a bully but gentle, not quarrelsome, not greedy—one who manages his own household competently, having his children under control with all dignity. (If anyone does not know how to manage his own household, how will he take care of God's church?) He must not be a new convert, or he might become conceited and fall into the condemnation of the Devil. Furthermore, he must have a good reputation among outsiders, so that he does not fall into disgrace and the Devil's trap. (1 Tim. 3:1–7)

Reflecting on this list, New Testament scholar D. A. Carson has observed that what's remarkable is how unremarkable the characteristics are. Paul does not ask for men who can preach to thousands, evangelize millions, and rescue orphans from burning buildings. Rather, he lists characteristics that are enjoined on all Christians—except for "able to teach" and "not a recent convert." Why would this be the case? Because an elder should model a life that is exemplary for other Christians. You wouldn't want an elder's pattern of life to be something that is unreachable, but something that can be followed.

Notice also, the characteristics are virtues that would commend an elder to outsiders, or that would have caused a man to be recognized as virtuous even by the surrounding culture of the time. There are other virtues, after all, that we would want to see in an elder, like regular Bible reading and prayer. But Paul mentioned neither of these. This tells us that we should not regard this list as exhaustive, but it also tells us that Paul is emphasizing things that even pagans would recognize as good. Contrast that with the evident ungodliness of some of the false teachers in the Ephesian church who jeopardized the whole way that God would be glorified through the church.

How do we find such leaders in our churches? We pray for God's wisdom. We study his Word, particularly these passages in 1 Timothy and Titus. And we look to affirm such gifts of Christ as he gives them. We should not be slower to recognize them than Christ gives them.

We should also not assume that because a man is a proven leader in the world, he is fit to lead a church. Too many churches fall into the trap of appointing men who have been successful in the business or professional community. How sad, then, to hear what Os Guinness heard from one Japanese businessman: "Whenever I meet a Buddhist leader, I meet a holy man. Whenever I meet a Christian leader, I meet a manager."[16]

Churches should search for men of character, reputation, ability to handle the Word, and fruitfulness. These qualities should mark the leaders of our church. They live not for themselves, but others. Thus, they are not lovers of money, but lovers of strangers—that's what "hospitable" literally means.

Historical Overview

All churches have had individuals who performed the functions of elders, even if they called them by other names. The two most common New Testament names for this office were *episcopos* (overseer) and *presbuteros* (elder).

When evangelicals today hear the word *elder*, they often think "Presbyterian." While it is historically accurate to associate elders with Presbyterians, it is not accurate to associate them exclusively with Presbyterians. The first Congregationalists in the sixteenth century taught that eldership was an office in a New Testament church. And elders could be found in Baptist churches in America throughout the eighteenth century and into the nineteenth century.[17] For instance, W. B. Johnson, the first president of the Southern Baptist

Convention, wrote a book on church life in which he strongly advocated the idea of a plurality of elders in one local church.

Whether through inattention to Scripture, or the pressure of life on the frontier (where churches sprang up at an amazing rate), the practice of cultivating such textured leadership declined in Baptist churches. But Baptist papers continued to call for reviving this biblical office. As late as the early twentieth century, Baptist publications referred to the leaders by the title of "elder."

Though this practice was somewhat unusual among Baptist churches in the twentieth century, there is now a growing trend back toward it—and for good reason. It was needed in New Testament churches, and it is needed now.

CHAPTER 4

What Do Elders Do?

We have seen who the elders are. What do they do?

Elders Pray

The elders of the church should pray for the members of the church (see James 5:14; Acts 6:4). God gives elders responsibility for a flock, and so they should pray for their flocks individually, collectively, and in the congregation.

Individually, I love the members of the local church I serve. Each morning, I pray name by name through a couple of pages of the church's membership directory.

Together in the elders' meetings in my church, our elders give significant time—perhaps as much as an hour out of a three-hour meeting—to praying for our members. We go name by name through a portion of the directory. We then pray for the sheep in particular trouble.

In the gatherings of my church, elders lead the way in adoring God for who he is in himself through prayers of praise.

They set a pattern of noticing God's faithfulness through prayers of thanksgiving, especially since elders are in a great position to see God's work. Elders should watch for the answers to prayer and point them out to the congregation.

They also set a pattern through corporate prayers of confession. They help the church recognize God's holiness by confessing sin. In private and in public they should examine themselves to see if they are in the faith (2 Cor. 13:5). Their explorations of their own hearts should cause the congregation to have a greater appreciation of God's mercy and grace, and also encourage others as they lead the congregation in confessing sins to God.

Intercessory prayer is perhaps the most basic ministry of the elder. In order to speak to men for God, elders must speak to God for men. They must be aware of the futility of all of their actions apart from the life-giving work of God's Spirit. Elders do and must pray.

Elders Preach and Teach

The other basic activity of elders is preaching and teaching the Word of God to the congregation.[18] A qualification of elders is that they must be able to teach because so much of what they do is teaching (see 1 Tim. 3:2). Elders teach by leading the meetings of the church. They teach by the way they give announcements or read Scripture. They teach by how they pray aloud in public. Certainly they teach when they lead a Sunday school class, whether for children or adults.

Elders teach the Word of God by preaching. Elders set aside to do this work full-time are wonderful gifts to the local church. But an elder does not need to be set aside full-time or be the main preaching pastor in order for his basic ministry to be teaching. Elders teach in their one-on-one conversations and in what they write. They teach in small group Bible studies and in evangelistic endeavors.

This is why elders must be men who devote themselves to knowing the Word of God. Psalms 1, 19, and 119 are good psalms for elders to study individually and together. Elders should also specially give themselves to figuring out and understanding important topics in the Bible and in life so that the members of the congregation will be protected, prepared, and equipped.

As elders teach, they reflect the manner in which the Good News came to their ears and hearts from the outside and saved them. Elders, too, speak God's truth to the ears of the congregation, and then they pray that God's Spirit would carry it the rest of the way into the hearts of the men and women in their charge.

Elders teach and preach God's Word.

Elders Shepherd

The most comprehensive word for what elders do is "shepherd" (Acts 20:28; 1 Pet. 5:2). In the New Testament's Greek, as in English, there is both a noun form and a verb form of the word *shepherd*. A shepherd (noun) is someone who shepherds (verb). And in Scripture this refers to activities like knowing, feeding, leading, and protecting.[19] In some ways, every Christian participates in shepherding (see Rom. 15:14). Yet some men are specially recognized and set apart for the work of shepherding a congregation. These are the elders in the congregation.

To shepherd is to care for those who don't belong to you, but for whom you are charged (see Luke 12:35–48). Think about what this means when someone joins a church. If you're an elder, you know that this person has been purchased by God, but he or she is your special responsibility. Hebrews 13:17 says that you will give an account to God for such individuals.

Elders therefore lead the way in rejoicing with these members, and mourning with them. Elders set a pattern for the members of caring when someone loses a job, or when someone is frustrated in his or her relationships. Elders are discontent when a member misunderstands God or his Word, and they give themselves to tending to such individuals.

Shepherding, like parenting, requires patience. This kind of work is not done in a single sermon or in a day. Sometimes, of course, God does cause breakthroughs in a single sermon or crucial conversation.

But usually the work of eldering is as repetitive and daily as walking the flock to a fresh field for grazing. It is like making the daily meals or taking the kids to school.

It seems that some of the most important work in shaping a congregation's character is the small, slow, repetitive acts of love and service that elders do. Teaching that Sunday school lesson again. Leading in prayer again. Answering that question for the tenth time. Or the one hundredth!

Shepherding also requires initiative. An elder cannot be passive, merely waiting for people to come with questions to answer or problems to solve. Elders need to ask, "How was the sermon for you?" "Do you want to have lunch?" "Do you know how so-and-so is doing?" "Do you understand what the Bible teaches about the Holy Spirit's work?" "Have you read this?" "Do you want to come hang out while I work on this Bible study?" "Do you want to go over my notes with me here to see if it makes sense, and to help me make it better?" "How is your father, your wife, your non-Christian colleague?" These and a thousand other initiatives can be used by God to shape, encourage, comfort, correct, or lead a sheep committed to one's elder-care.

Elders Watch over Themselves and Their Families

One duty even the best elders may sometimes neglect is the care of their own souls. But Paul instructs the Ephesian elders to "pay careful attention to yourselves" (Acts 20:28 ESV).

Brother elder, this means that the time you spend daily in God's Word and in prayer is certainly for yourself, but it is also part of the role God has given you in the life of your local church. It's like the flight attendant on an airplane who instructs you to put the oxygen mask over your own face first in the case of an emergency; then assist anyone travelling with you. So it is with you. Make sure you're breathing! Then help others to breathe.

I've sometimes joked that I'm not sure I'm a good enough Christian *not* to be a pastor. What I mean is, the regular rhythm of teaching, preparing, and taking responsibility to pray for and love this group of people are all helpful expectations for me. I like being yoked up. It helps me to do not just what is useful for others, but for myself as well. Conversely, what is useful for me helps me to continue being of use to others.

This means, among other things, that my family needs to understand that there will be costs to them because of my role, but also that I know that I have a unique responsibility for them. This congregation can get another pastor, other elders. My children cannot get another father or my wife another husband. I have a unique lifelong role with them. While I've failed at fulfilling this responsibility many times, I've never denied it. I have always recognized this, and that means that I have worked hard to make sure that my wife understands that the sacrifices that she or the family make for our church are sacrifices that I am leading us to make—I who in theory and practice treasure my family. I work to build up that trust in my loving leadership at home.

Elders Exercise Oversight

As they care for themselves, elders can then care for others by exercising oversight. Paul's words to the Ephesian elders are instructive: "Pay careful attention to yourselves and to all the flock, of which the Holy Spirit has made you overseers, to care for the church of God, which he obtained with his own blood" (Acts 20:28 ESV).

Elders exercise oversight in all sorts of ways. They do it by concerning themselves with the gospel work that the congregation sponsors. They meet with missionaries, and maybe they even travel to where the missionaries live and work.

Elders exercise oversight by meeting with the members of the congregation in their homes, and maybe even at their places of work.

They look after their members' life and doctrine. After all, they have an authority given by God to exercise for the members' good.

Elders exercise oversight by examining individuals for membership and then recommending them to the congregation. Sometimes this means slowing down someone's application to join the church because they want to help the individual understand something better, resolve questions, or sort out some area of his or her life.

Elders exercise oversight when they lead the congregation to exclude from membership someone who has decided that he loves his sin more than he loves Christ.

Elders can exercise oversight by composing and submitting a budget annually to the congregation.

They counsel each other on difficult pastoral situations in members' lives.

They pray together.

They continually search for whom God is raising up as elders or deacons.

They invite hurting or struggling sheep to meet with them to pray for them in their trial or sickness, to hear about their struggles with sin, or to advise them in their desire to take the gospel overseas.

In all these ways and more, elders seek to fulfill Peter's exhortation, "shepherd the flock of God, that is among you, exercising oversight, not under compulsion, but willingly, as God would have you" (1 Pet. 5:2 ESV).

Elders Set a Good Example

One of the best ways a man can be a good elder is to be a good example to the flock. Think of Paul's description to Titus of an elder, and consider how they are to be models for others:

> For an overseer, as God's administrator, must be blameless, not arrogant, not hot-tempered, not addicted to wine, not a bully,

not greedy for money, but hospitable, loving what is good,
sensible, righteous, holy, self-controlled, holding to the faithful
message as taught, so that he will be able both to encourage
with sound teaching and to refute those who contradict it.
(Titus 1:7–9)

Why are elders or pastors to be all of those things? Because part of oversight is showing the way. They lead the way as disciples. By instructing, they show how to instruct. By being faithful, they show what it looks like to be faithful. They obey Peter's instruction to be examples to the flock (1 Pet. 5:3).

Elders Raise up Elders

Finally, elders continually work to make themselves redundant by raising up other elders. In a sense, this is just a part of the "making disciples" mandate. They teach and train so that others will grow toward maturity and will teach and train in turn.

Consider how Paul instructs Timothy: "And what you have heard from me in the presence of many witnesses, commit to faithful men who will be able to teach others also" (2 Tim. 2:2). Paul (generation 1) taught Timothy (generation 2). He wants Timothy to commit those lessons to faithful men (generation 3). And he wants those faithful men to teach others also (generation 4). How many of us have our spiritual great-grandchildren in mind, like Paul! A congregation where more and more men are being cultivated and grown up as elders is a healthy and powerful congregation.

In summary, elders must know their sheep and serve them. Godly elders lead their sheep and feed them. They give themselves to ruling well and guarding them carefully. They seek out the lowly and despised. They train those gifted to teach others. In all of this, they follow the example of Christ, the Good Shepherd who loses none of his sheep.

CHAPTER 5

How Do the Elders Relate to Staff, Deacons, and "the Pastor"?

If elders are primarily responsible for teaching and oversight, how should elders relate to church staff, the deacons, and any senior or lead pastor? I think it's important for us to distinguish each of these roles and know who's responsible for what. What work and decisions belong to the elders? The staff? The deacons? The whole church?

Relationship of Elders and Church Staff

Many contemporary churches confuse elders with the church staff. Some staff are pastors. Some staff are not. Either way, the staff are the people whom the church has set aside full- or part-time to work for the church. Often they are the people most directly familiar with what is going on day-to-day. They must have a certain degree of godliness and maturity or they should never have been hired in the first place. Those who are pastors may have attended seminary, but maybe not.

If a man on staff has the title of "pastor," he is also an elder. Every pastor is an elder because the words in Scripture are interchangeable, as I mentioned earlier. So my own church would not give the title, say, of "youth pastor" to someone who was not also an elder. Of the twenty-four elders currently recognized by our church, only six are employed by the church.

That said, we have a number of men—typically younger—who are doing pastoral work, but they have not yet been affirmed as elders. These "pastoral assistants" provide wonderful care for us in everything from teaching to visiting. We also have a godly woman who directs children's ministry, as well as administrative staff generally.

How then do the elders and the staff relate? Since the elders as a whole possess oversight over the congregation, larger decisions of oversight must remain with them. The staff, then, are responsible for executing these decisions. To be sure, the elders as a whole often rely upon the staff elders for some measure of guidance on decisions belonging to all of them. After all, the staff elders have all week to pursue this work.

Relationship of Elders and Deacons

In practice if not in doctrine, many churches also confuse the New Testament roles of deacon and elder.

If you compare the lists of elder and deacon qualifications in 1 Timothy 3, most noticeable are not the differences, but the similarities. Both elders and deacons need to be reputable, blameless, trusted, monogamous, sober, temperate, and generous individuals. Indeed, so similar are these two lists that it's striking the early Christians should so clearly recognize two separate bodies of leaders. The main difference between the two lists is that an elder must be "an able teacher."

We saw the root of this distinction in Acts 6. The apostles observed that it would not be right for them "to give up preaching about God to handle financial matters" (v. 2). They wanted to devote themselves "to prayer and to the preaching ministry" (v. 4). The chosen seven, meanwhile, were set aside to wait on tables. Likewise, the ministry of the Word of God is central to the responsibility of the elders, both in their public handling of the Word and in their lives. The deacons, meanwhile, should concern themselves with the practical details of church life: administration, maintenance, and the care of church members with physical needs—all in order to promote the unity of the church and the ministry of the Word.

Elders are deacons of preaching and prayer. The deacons are deacons of the practical and physical.

The deacons, therefore, should not act as a separate power bloc or second house of the legislature through which bills need to be passed. If the elders say, "Let's drive to Pittsburgh," it's not up to the deacons to come back and say, "No, let's drive to Philadelphia instead." They can legitimately come back and say, "Our engine won't get us to Pittsburgh. Perhaps we should reconsider." That's very helpful. But in general their job is to support the destination set by the elders.

It would be to the great benefit of many churches to again distinguish the role of elder from that of deacon.

Relationship of the Elders and "the Pastor"

Does the Bible teach that there should be a senior pastor-figure among the elders? The answer to that question is "No, not directly." Having said that, I do think that we can discern in the Scriptures a distinct role among the elders for one who is the primary public teacher. Let me give you four New Testament glimpses of this kind of role:

1. Some elder-types moved from place to place (like Timothy and Titus), while some didn't. So Timothy came from outside, while others were appointed within his local congregation.
2. Some elders were supported full-time by the flock (see 1 Tim. 5:17–18; Phil. 4:15–18), while others worked at another job. It seems unlikely that everyone Titus appointed for the churches in Crete could have been paid full-time.
3. Paul wrote to Timothy alone with instructions for the church, even though we know from Acts that there were other elders in the Ephesian church. Timothy seems to have possessed a unique function among them.

4. Finally, the letters of Jesus to the seven churches in Revelation 2 and 3 are addressed to the messenger (singular) of each of these churches.

None of these are airtight commands for churches today. But they are descriptions consistent with our practice of setting aside one elder, supporting him financially, and giving him the primary teaching responsibility in the church. As he teaches faithfully, he will naturally accrue authority to himself, which in turn will afford him with a "first among equals" role among the elders for establishing the direction of the church. And since the elders have set him aside full-time for this work, they should look for such leadership.

That said, the preacher or pastor is fundamentally just one of the elders. And all of them possess Holy Spirit-assigned oversight, such that he possesses only one vote along with each of them.

Such a plurality makes leadership more rooted and permanent and allows for continuity in leadership when the senior pastor departs. It encourages the church to take more responsibility for raising up its own members and helps make the church less dependent on its employees. The plurality-of-elder model, in other words, is nothing less than a call for discipling and raising up leaders.

As a senior pastor, probably the single most helpful thing to my pastoral ministry has been the recognition of the other elders. Their service has had immense benefits. They round out my gifts, make up for some of my deficiencies, supplement my judgment, and create support in the congregation for decisions, leaving me less exposed to unjust criticism. My church, too, has benefited immensely from these men as they have shepherded their souls.

CHAPTER 6

How Do the Elders Relate to the Congregation?

So far we have considered the work of elders and deacons and how elders relate to different parts of the body. But what exactly does elder leadership mean in the context of congregationalism?[20]

What Is Congregationalism?

Let me start by answering: What is congregationalism? Congregationalism is simply the understanding that the last and final court of appeal in the local church is not the bishop of Rome or Constantinople or Washington. It is not some international body or some national assembly, conference, or convention. It is not the president of a denomination or the chairman of a board of trustees. It is not a regional synod or ministerial association. It is not a group of elders inside the local church, or the pastor. The last and final court of appeal in a matter of the life of the local church is the local congregation itself.

This seems to be evidenced by the New Testament in matters of doctrine and discipline, as well as in matters of admission of members and the settling of differences between them.

Disputes. In Matthew 18:15–17, Jesus told of a dispute between brothers. Notice what court is the final judicatory. It is not a bishop, a presbytery, or the pastors. It is "the church" (v. 17). The whole local congregation must be the final court of appeals.

Doctrine. In Galatians 1:6–9, Paul calls on congregations of fairly young Christians to sit in judgment of angelic and apostolic preachers (even himself!) if they should preach any other gospel than the one that the Galatians had accepted. He makes this point again in 2 Timothy 4:3 when he counsels Timothy and the church in Ephesus on the best way to handle false teachers.

Discipline. In 1 Corinthians 5, Paul appeals to the whole Corinthian congregation (not just to the elders) to act to exclude a man who is living contrary to his profession of faith. In matters of church discipline, the congregation as a whole is the final court held out in Scripture.

Membership. In 2 Corinthians 2:6–8 (NIV), Paul appeals to the action of the majority in excluding a man from membership, and now he wants them to restore the man to membership: "The punishment inflicted on him by the majority is sufficient. Now instead, you ought to forgive and comfort him, so that he will not be overwhelmed by excessive sorrow. I urge you, therefore, to reaffirm your love for him." In matters of church membership, the congregation as a whole must be the final court.

How much further a congregation decides to involve itself corporately in decisions about the leadership, the staff, and the budget is then a matter of prudence and discretion. Neither nominating committees nor trustees are found on the pages of the New Testament. You will look in vain for finance committees or small group leadership teams. Belief in the sufficiency of Scripture, however, doesn't forbid such structures; it just relativizes their authority.

Keep in mind also that the congregation is not always right. When Paul wrote to Timothy, his disciple and the pastor of the church in Ephesus, he described the coming evil days "when people will not put up with sound doctrine. Instead, to suit their own desires, they will gather around them a great number of teachers to say what their itching ears want to hear" (2 Tim. 4:3). Congregationalism is biblical, but the congregation is not inerrant. In history, we can consider the congregation that fired Jonathan Edwards. They had every biblical right to have that kind of authority, but I think they were wrong to use it to fire Edwards. Even rightful authority established by God in this fallen world will err.

Trusting and Obeying Leaders

So if congregationalism affirms that the church is the final court of appeals, how do we put that together with verses like Hebrews 13:17? "Obey your leaders and submit to them, for they keep watch over your souls as those who will give an account, so that they can do this with joy and not with grief, for that would be unprofitable for you." We are not accustomed to using words like "obey" and "submit," but the New Testament applies them to people in society and at work, at home and in our marriages, and in the church. Obeying and trusting our leaders does require, on our part, a certain amount of trust.

It has been said that trust must be earned. I understand what is meant. But that attitude is at best only half true. The kind of trust that we are called to give to our fellow imperfect humans in this life, be they family or friends, employers or government officials, or even leaders in the church, can never finally be earned. It must be given as a gift—a gift in faith, more in trust of the God who gives than of those whom we see as God's gifts to us. It is a serious spiritual deficiency in a church either to have leaders who are untrustworthy or members who are incapable of trusting.

You as a church member either need to trust your leaders or replace them. But don't say that you acknowledge them and then not follow them. If you disagree with the elders on a recommendation, have a good reason. Go and talk with them about it. Other than the Bible, you are the elders' main source of information about you!

Rather than distrusting church leaders, let me encourage you to talk behind your elders' backs: meet in secret and plot to encourage your leaders. Strategize to make the church leaders' work not burdensome, but a joy. This, the writer to the Hebrews says, will make your leaders a blessing to you.

5 Characteristics of the Relationship

Both elders and members serve one another and depend upon God. Let me summarize this relationship with five characteristics.

1. **Clear Recognition.** The congregation should recognize elders as gifts from God for their good. They revoke their duties to teach and lead only when the elders act contrary to the Scriptures. For their part, the elders must recognize the God-given authority of the congregation.

2. **Heart-felt Trust.** The church should trust, protect, respect, and honor its elders. "The elders who direct the affairs of the church well are worthy of double honor," says Paul (1 Tim. 5:17 NIV). And members should "regard [their leaders] very highly in love because of their work" (1 Thess. 5:13). The elders should direct the affairs of the church, and the church should submit to their leadership.

3. **Evident Godliness.** We have seen the emphasis in Paul's letters to Timothy and Titus on the elders being "blameless" (see Titus 1:6). The elder, then, must be willing for his life to be open to inspection and for his home to be actively open to outsiders, giving hospitality and enfolding others into his family's life.

4. **Sincere Carefulness.** The elders' use of authority should demonstrate their understanding that the church belongs not to them, but to Christ. Christ has purchased the church with his own blood. Therefore the elders should cherish the church, treat it carefully and gently, and lead it faithfully and purely for the glory of God. The elders will give an account to Christ for their stewardship.

5. **Beneficial Results.** Authority used well benefits those led by it. So it is in a home and in our relationship with God. And so it is in the congregation. The congregation will benefit as God builds it up through the teachers he gives. Satan's lie—that authority can never be

trusted because it is always tyrannical and oppressive—will be subverted by the elders' benevolent exercise of authority.

Hebrews 13:17, quoted earlier, promises that leaders will give an account for how they lead, and it promises members that not following their leaders will prove "unprofitable." Scripture calls both leaders and members to account.

When Edward Griffin (1770–1837) was retiring from the church he had served so well for many years, he exhorted the congregation on how to regard not just the pastor. His words also instruct us in how to cherish all of those whom God has given us as elders:

> For your own sake, and your children's sake, cherish and
> revere him whom you have chosen to be your pastor. Already
> he loves you; and he will soon love you as "bone of his bone,
> and flesh of his flesh." It will be equally your duty and your
> interest to make his labors as pleasant to him as possible. Do
> not demand too much. Do not require visits too frequent.
> Should he spend, in this way, half of the time which some
> demand, he must wholly neglect his studies, if not sink early
> under the burden. Do not report to him all the unkind things
> which may be said against him; nor frequently, in his presence,
> allude to opposition, if opposition should arise. Though he is a
> minister of Christ, consider that he has the feelings of a man.[21]

Congregationalism—Why It Is Important

Why does all this matter? First, we should trust the structures that God has created and trust his wisdom in doing so.

Second, the verdict of history is in. No polity prevents churches from all error, from declension, and from sterility, but the more centralized polities seem to have a worse track record in maintaining a faithful, vital, evangelical witness than congregational churches. The papacy has wrought havoc on self-confessed Christians. Bishops have hardly done better. Even assemblies, conferences, presbyteries, synods, and sessions, when they have moved from being advisors to being sole deciders, have overstepped their scripturally warranted authority and have brought more trouble than help.

Could it be that the gospel itself is so simple and clear, and the relationship that we have with God by the Holy Spirit's action in the new birth so real, that the collection of those who believe the gospel and who know God are simply the best guardians of that gospel? Isn't that what we see in the Scriptures?[22]

Elder-led congregationalism, concludes Jonathan Leeman, is a "gospel powerhouse." It "guards the gospel, matures the Christian disciple, strengthens the whole church, fortifies its holy integrity and witness, and equips the congregation to better love their neighbors in word and deed."

CHAPTER 7

Who Are the Members?

Since the elders lead in the context of congregationalism, we have to ask finally who the members are.

The whole idea of church membership seems counterproductive to many today. Isn't it unfriendly, and maybe even elitist, to say that some are in and others out? In fact, I'm convinced that getting this right is a key step toward revitalizing our churches, evangelizing our nation, furthering the cause of Christ around the world, and so bringing glory to God!

American evangelicals are in pretty desperate need of reconsidering this topic, especially my own fellowship of churches, the Southern Baptist Convention. According to one Southern Baptist study a few years ago, the typical Southern Baptist church has 233 members with 70 present at the Sunday morning worship service. My question is this: where are the other 163 members? What does this convey about Christianity to the world around us?

What Is a Church?

We start with the question, "What is a church?" A church is not a building. Fundamentally, a church is its members. It is a regular assembly of people who profess and give evidence that they have been saved by God's grace alone through faith alone in Christ alone to the glory of

God alone. The early Christians didn't have any buildings for almost three hundred years after the church began. From the earliest of times, though, local churches were congregations of specific people. Certain people would have been known to make up this assembly, and others known as outside of it. Thus the censures taught by Jesus in Matthew 18 and Paul in 1 Corinthians 5 envision an individual being excluded.

The idea of a defined community of people is central to God's action in both the Old and the New Testaments. He separated and distinguished Noah and his family. Then Abraham and his descendants. Then the nation of Israel. And now the church in the New Testament. God has always maintained a distinct and separate people in order to display his character. Therefore he has intended for a sharp, bright line to distinguish those who specially belong to him from those who do not.

This concept of the church as a gathered community is something that has distinguished Baptist Christians from many others. At the time of the Reformation the relationship between state and church was both close and complicated. It was assumed that everyone born within the bounds of a certain political jurisdiction should be able to be a member of the state church. Baptists then helped to recover believer's baptism and the idea of the church as a congregation of those professing and evidencing regeneration.

The church is not finally something for people with the right family by natural descent or by virtue of one's citizenship in a nation. No, the New Testament teaches that the church is for believers. So we advocate laws in this land that provide the kind of freedom for that church to be able to operate in liberty. Baptists do not, then, advocate for a new established church in America; indeed, we are its firmest foes. Our very understanding of the church will not allow that. We instead advocate the evangelization of the nation and world through churches that freely cooperate together in the gospel of Jesus Christ.

Marks of Church Membership

How do we know who is and who is not a member of a particular church?

First, to be a member of a church, you must be baptized as a believer. In Matthew 28, Jesus commands everyone who would follow him to profess their faith publicly in baptism. Through baptism we formally identify with his name. Throughout the book of Acts, then, the disciples understood and obeyed this command. When Paul wrote the church in Rome, therefore, he simply assumed he was writing a group of baptized people (Rom. 6:3–4).

Second, to be a member of a church, you must regularly receive the Lord's Supper. Through the Supper we share in the one body of Christ and declare his death (1 Cor. 10:16–17). If baptism is the sign of the new covenant, the Lord's Supper is its meal of remembrance. We eat and drink "in remembrance" of him. For more on baptism and the Lord's Supper, see Bobby Jamieson's two books on these topics in the Church Basics series.

Third, to be a member of a church, you must regularly gather with the church. This is perhaps our most basic ministry to each other. The author of Hebrews commands, "And let us be concerned about one another in order to promote love and good works, not staying away from our worship meetings, as some habitually do, but encouraging each other, and all the more as you see the day drawing near" (10:24–25).

The New Testament calls the church a spiritual household and each of us the stones (1 Pet. 2:5). It calls the church a body and each of us the members (1 Cor. 12). It also says we are sheep in a flock and branches on a vine (John 10:16; 15:5). Biblically, a Christian must be a member of a church. And membership is not simply a name on a piece of paper or our declaration of affection toward the place we grew up. It must reflect a living commitment and a regular attendance or it is worthless. Indeed, it is worse than worthless; it is dangerous.

Uninvolved "members" confuse both real members and non-Christians about what it means to be a Christian. And we "active" members do the voluntarily "inactive" members no service when we allow them to remain members of the church since membership provides the church's corporate endorsement of a person's salvation. Please understand: church membership is a church's corporate testimony to an individual's salvation. So how can a congregation honestly testify that someone it never sees is faithfully running the race?

In my own church, we constantly try to watch for who has slipped away from attending. If they are able to attend, we encourage them to come back or join another church. If they refuse, we move toward discipline; which brings us to our next point.

Fourth, being a church member means submitting to the accountability and discipline of a church. Teachers teach and correct mistakes. Doctors prescribe healthy living and fight against disease. Christian discipleship, too, involves formative discipline (teaching) and corrective discipline. We discipline one another informally in private with words of correction. We do it formally and publicly when a person refuses to repent. Jesus commanded it. Paul commanded it. And churches from these earliest times practiced it. See Jonathan Leeman's book on this topic in the Church Basics series.

Fifth and finally, love is a mark of church membership. Jesus told his disciples, "I give you a new command: Love one another. Just as I have loved you, you must also love one another. By this all people will know that you are My disciples, if you have love for one another" (John 13:34–35). You cannot call yourself a Christian without being in committed loving relationships with other Christians. John warns, "If anyone says, 'I love God,' yet hates his brother, he is a liar. For anyone who does not love his brother, whom he has seen, cannot love God, whom he has not seen" (1 John 4:20). Given our propensity to deceive ourselves, and to overestimate our own goodness, thank God that he has given us other saints to check our own pride and blindness!

Many other things flow out of the loving commitment we make to one another in a local church. For example, we ask members of our church to sign a statement of faith and a church covenant. We expect that members will pray for the church, that they will give financially to support the church, and that they will be involved in ministries of the church. But it all begins with baptism, the Lord's Supper, attendance, discipline, and love.

Why Join a Church?

Church membership is a crucial part of following Christ as a disciple. It will not save you any more than your good works, education, culture, friendships, contributions, or baptism will save you. But joining a church is what members of Christ's body do. Don't say you belong to *the* church if you won't join *a* church.

Let me give you six reasons to join a church that preaches the gospel and models Christian living.

1. To Assure Yourself

You should not join a church to be saved, but to help you make certain you are saved. Remember what Jesus said: "Whoever has my commands and obeys them, he is the one who loves me. He who loves me will be loved by my Father, and I too will love him and show myself to him" (John 14:21 NIV).

In joining the church, we put ourselves in a position where we ask our brothers and sisters to hold us accountable to live by what we speak. We ask them to encourage us with how they see God working in our lives, and to challenge us when we may be moving away from obedience to him. Your membership in a local church is that congregation's public testimony that your life gives evidence of regeneration. It doesn't save, but it reflects salvation. And if there is no reflection, how can we be sure about our claims of salvation?

In becoming a member of a church, we grasp hands with each other to know and be known by each other.

2. To Be Equipped for Ministry

Paul says, "[Christ] personally gave some to be apostles, some prophets, some evangelists, some pastors and teachers, for the training of the saints in the work of ministry, to build up the body of Christ" (Eph. 4:11–12). Notice two things here. First, church leaders equip us. Second, they equip us for the work of the ministry of building up the body of Christ.

In other words, we join churches in order to get equipped to do the ministry work to which we are all called. What a gift church leaders are! Join a church for the sake of its leaders. Support them as they equip and prepare you.

3. To Edify the Church

If we join in order to be equipped, we also join to be equipped *for* building up the church. A third reason for joining the church, then, is the edification or building up of the church. Joining a church will help us counter our wrong individualism and discover the corporate nature of Christianity. The New Testament teaches that a Christian life involves care and concern for each other. That is part of what it means to be a Christian. And though we do it imperfectly, we should be committed to do this. We intend to encourage even baby steps in righteousness, love, selflessness, and Christlikeness.

In my church's membership class, I often tell the story of a friend who worked for a campus Christian ministry while attending a church in which I was a member. He would always slip in right after the hymns, sit there for the sermon, and then leave. I asked him one day why he didn't come for the whole service. "Well," he said, "I don't get anything out of the rest of it."

"Have you ever thought about joining the church?" I responded.

He thought that was just an absurd question: "Why would I join the church? If I join them, I think they would just slow me down spiritually." When he said this, I wondered what he understood being a Christian meant.

I replied, "Have you ever considered that maybe God wants you to link arms with those other people? Sure, they might slow you down, but you might help to speed them up. Maybe that's part of God's plan for us as we live together as Christians!"

4. To Evangelize the World

You should also join a local church for the sake of evangelizing the world. A local church is, by nature, a missionary organization. Together we can better spread the gospel at home and abroad. We do this by our words, as we share the message of the Good News and help one another to share. And we do this by our lives together. Together we present a corporate testimony to the life-changing power of our words. That corporate testimony includes everything from our shared hospitality with each other to our meeting the physical needs of orphans, the sick, children, and the disadvantaged.

Through the fellowship of multiple churches, we help spread the gospel around the world, and we provide millions of dollars and thousands of volunteers to help those with immediate physical needs like disaster relief, education, and countless other ministries. We are imperfect, but if God's Spirit is genuinely at work in us, he will use our lives and words to help demonstrate the truth of his gospel. This is the special privilege of the church now—to be part of God's plan to take his gospel to the world.

5. To Expose False Gospels

God intends us to be together in this way to expose false gospels. It is through our coming together as Christians that we show the world what Christianity really is. In our churches, we debunk messages and images that purport to be biblical Christianity but are not.

There are many bad, confusing, distorted witnesses that have raised themselves up as Christian "churches." Part of the church's mission is to defend the true gospel and to prevent and dismantle perversions of it.

6. To Glorify God

Finally, a Christian should join a church for the glory of God. Peter wrote to some early Christians, "Live such good lives among the pagans that, though they accuse you of doing wrong, they may see your good deeds and glorify God on the day he visits us" (1 Pet. 2:12 NIV). Amazing, isn't it? God will receive the glory for our good works! You can tell that Peter had heard the teaching of his Master, who said at the Sermon on the Mount, "Let your light shine before men, that they may see your good works and give glory to your Father in heaven" (Matt. 5:16).

If that is true of our lives individually, it shouldn't be surprising to find that God's Word says the same about our lives together in churches. The world will identify us as Christians by our love for one another: "All people will know that you are My disciples, if you have love for one another" (John 13:35). Our lives together mark us out as belonging to him, bringing him praise and glory.

So my Christian friend, do not merely attend a church, but join a church. Link arms with other Christians. Find a church you can join, and do it so that non-Christians will hear and see the gospel, so that weak Christians will be cared for, so that strong Christians will channel their energies in a good way, so that church leaders will be encouraged and helped, so that God will be glorified.

A Display of God's Glory

Paul's first letter to the Corinthians is wonderful to meditate on if you want to understand what life together as a church entails. You will find that churches should be marked especially by holiness, unity, and love.

Why should churches be like this? Because the character of the church should reflect the character of God. We should be holy, united, and loving because God is holy, One, and loving.

Holy, One, and Loving

First, we should be holy in the sense of being strange to the world, but special to God, set apart to him, pure. Holiness should be an attribute that marks the church—a trademark, common among us, typical. When someone considers our particular church, they should think, *That is a holy community*—not meaning a bunch of self-righteous, prudish people, but a community of people whose hearts are singularly set on Christ and his glory, which results in a better, more humane, more God-honoring way of living. That's one reason why the church leader's work of shepherding and teaching is important. We are to be holy because God is holy.

Second, we should be united because God is One. After hearing of the Corinthian church's divisions and factions, Paul asks, "Is Christ divided?" (1 Cor. 1:13). What a fascinating question! The powerful theological assumption behind it is that the church is the body of Christ: "You are the body of Christ, and each one of you is a part of it" (1 Cor. 12:27 NIV). Where do you think Paul got that idea? I think he got it in the very hour he was converted. Remember how Jesus stopped Paul on the road to Damascus? Jesus didn't say, "Saul, Saul, why are you persecuting Christians?" or "Saul, Saul, why are you persecuting the church?" No. He said, "Saul, Saul, why are you persecuting Me?" (Acts 9:4). This is how closely Jesus relates to his church. He views it as his body. And so we are to be one. Our disunity lies about Jesus and what he is like.

Like holiness, unity should be a hallmark of the church. Our unity should transcend the old divisions of Jew and Gentile (1 Cor. 7:19), along with every other worldly division. How tragic, then, when our churches find their identity in other things. We become *the church of this pastor,* or *of this style of music,* or *of home schoolers,* or *of Democrats*, or *of the blue carpet.* This is why Paul was so upset by the report of divisions in the church. Even at the feast of their unity—the Lord's Supper—they were divided. Church leaders, however, should lead us toward such unity. The church is to be united.

Finally, we should be loving because God is loving. Brides like to have 1 Corinthians 13 read in their weddings, but fundamentally the Bible's great love chapter is about God and about the church. God's love is patient, kind, long-suffering, does not rejoice in evil, but delights in truth. So should ours be. Spiritual maturity, says Paul, is demonstrated in love. And it is the greatest gift. For that reason Paul wrote back in chapter 8, "We know that 'We all possess knowledge.' Knowledge puffs up, but love builds up" (8:1 NIV). Chapters 8 through 14 then provide a long excursion on letting love govern what we should do. And all our gifts and ministries and work together "must be done for the strengthening of the church" (14:26). Paul then summarizes in chapter 16, "Your every action must be done with love" (v. 14). Consider, after all, the love that Christ has shown by pouring out his blood and by offering up his body for us (11:23–26). The church is to be loving because God is loving—most wonderfully demonstrated in the gospel.

The church should be a display of God's holiness, unity, and love in the midst of this messed up, sinful, selfish world. Are we that? Does your church display the character of God? Too many churches today present a version of Christianity in which all sufferings are accounted for, all sacrifices rewarded, and all mysteries explained in this life. But this is not the gospel that Paul taught. In fact, this is not the gospel of our Lord Christ. And this must not be the gospel of our churches. If you evaluate a Christian's life this side of eternity, it will not add up. Christ's didn't; Paul's didn't. Ours shouldn't either (see 1 Cor. 15:17–19).

One of God's Chief Pieces of Evidence

Do you see what God is doing in the church? God is "choosing the lowly things of this world and the despised things—and the things that are not, so that no one may boast before him" (1 Cor. 1:28–29 NIV). God chooses weak and sinful people like you and me because he does not in any way want to obscure himself!

At a conference I attended a number of years ago, I heard Pastor Mark Ross make the point: "We are one of God's chief pieces of evidence." He continued, "Paul's great concern for the church is that the church manifest and display the glory of God, thus vindicating God's character against all the slander of demonic realms, the slander that God is not worth living for. God has entrusted to his church the glory of His own name. The circumstances of your life are the God-given occasion of your displaying and manifesting the attributes of God."

If we're not careful, our individualism can be used to harbor a sub-Christian holiness that tolerates sin. Our selfishness can lead us to a sub-Christian unity that papers over disunity about the gospel, and unites around other, lesser things. Even our flesh can know a sub-Christian love that is mere sentiment, having a family feeling because we've all been together so long. But none of these things should characterize our churches primarily because all of these things lie about God. They misrepresent his character. True holiness will include discipline. True unity will be only around Christ—and the diversity of the church will give evidence to this. And true love will go deeper than sentiment, beyond natural bounds. It will go out to the stranger for Christ's sake. This is how God's glory is displayed in the church. This is the only way a church will truly prosper.

So how do we display God's glory? By organizing our churches after the pattern he has shown us in his Word. By living for him with lives of holiness, unity, and love. This is to what the church should be devoted. Are you?

Elders: Leading and Setting the Pattern

In our present day as Western culture turns increasingly against Christianity, Christians need more than soaring sermons and thundering denunciations. They need incarnated witnesses to the glory of Christ. They need men who set the pattern of holiness, unity, and love. They need men who lead the way in swimming upstream, not floating downstream with the culture.

Not only that, they benefit from having not just one example of such a man in their churches. They benefit from God's provision of multiple elders, each of whom will, according to his own gifting, give careful, faithful, brave servant-leadership. "Remember your leaders who have spoken God's word to you. As you carefully observe the outcome of their lives, imitate their faith" (Heb. 13:7).

I first visited our congregation on Capitol Hill in the summer of 1993. I told the pulpit search committee openly of my belief in the Bible's teaching on a plural eldership. They were surprised, and, I think, a little put off. After teaching on the subject from time to time for a few years, we finally adopted a new constitution and our first set of elders in 1998.

For the last seventeen years, the brothers with whom I have been privileged to serve have given thousands of hours of their time to prayer, discussion, discipling, teaching, and shepherding the flock along with me. They have made up for some of my deficiencies. They have encouraged and corrected me. They have made what could be a very lonely job into a joy and delight. And our congregation has flourished in no small part, under God, due to their work. Thank goodness I am not the only one called to lead and set the pattern of holiness, unity, and love. How limited the church's picture of these things would be!

The Work to Be Done

There is much more work that needs to be done in Baptist churches around the world. The practice of membership in so many churches falls woefully short of the biblical picture. This, in turn, tarnishes our witness to the gospel and hinders our evangelism and discipling. Bloated membership lists, plummeting baptismal ages, irregular attendance, and the absence of church discipline mark too many of our churches. The changes needed for us to bear a distinct witness of life and light to our dark and dying day are great.

One of the greatest helps we could give to faithful pastors and to churches are groups of qualified men—men who are members of the church but largely not employed by it—to serve as elders. In fact, they really aren't our gifts to give. We can only recognize them. Jesus gives such gifts:

> Now grace was given to each one of us according to the measure of the Messiah's gift. For it says: When He ascended on high, He took prisoners into captivity; He gave gifts to people....
>
> And He personally gave some to be apostles, some prophets, some evangelists, some pastors and teachers for the training of the saints in the work of ministry, to build up the body of

Christ, until we all reach unity in the faith and in the knowledge of God's Son, growing into a mature man with a stature measured by Christ's fullness. (Eph. 4:7–8, 11–13)

Whether you are a church leader or member, what are you doing to recognize and honor and harness these amazing gifts?

APPENDIX

Deacon/Deaconess Job Descriptions

Here is a sample of several deacon/deaconess positions at Capitol Hill Baptist Church and their various responsibilities:

Deacon of Bookstall

This deacon maintains a database of bookstall holdings, recruits and trains volunteers to staff the bookstall, and handles matters relating to bookstall transactions.

Duties:

- Oversee bookstall holdings.
- Recruit and train volunteers to serve customers after Sunday AM/PM services and Wednesday night PM Study and Henry Forums in the following ways:
  - Meet and greet visitors in the bookstall area.
  - Take orders of books for sale at the bookstall.
  - Take special orders of CDs.
  - Record and maintain records of sales.
  - Send reminders for customers to pick up ordered items.
  - Re-stock shelves with free 9Marks literature.

- Submit sales summaries and money to CHBC staff member at the closing of bookstall.
- Notify CD Ministry regarding requests for special orders.
- Recruit and train volunteers to take weekly inventory.
- Price and shelve new inventory as needed.
- Maintain records of orders, work within a yearly budget.
- Interact with CD Ministry regarding CD orders.
- Order books to restock sold items.

Deacon of Budget

This deacon is responsible for coordinating the annual budget process by drafting a proposed budget with the assistance of the elders, other deacons, and the church administrator.

The budget process begins in May when the elders propose an amount for the church's spending on missions for the following year. The church administrator provides the deacon of budget with projected church expenses for facilities and administration.

Duties:

- Consult with the other deacons and the appropriate church members to determine requested expenses for each ministry for the following year.
- Interview the church staff to determine a proposed amount for church staff salaries and other staff expenses.
- Determine whether the church is able to meet the proposed budget through both income and expense projections. If he determines expenses will exceed income, he must inform the elders and return the proposed budget to them with suggested revisions.
- Answer any question by the congregation once the elders approve and propose the budget.

Deacon of Children's Ministry

These deacons are responsible for ensuring the cleanliness and order of the children's ministry areas, administratively overseeing compliance with CHBC policies, conducting training, and recording and scheduling the work of children's ministry volunteers.

Duties:

- Ensure safety and cleanliness of rooms before each service. This includes, but is not limited to, making sure age-appropriate toys are in each section, floor to ceiling beams are blocked, blind cords are up, and outlets are covered.
- Return washed toys to toy bins before each service.
- Oversee check-in and check-out of all children to and from the nursery and toddler rooms before and after each service.
- Ensure compliance with the child protection policy concerning staff-to-child ratios at each service.
- Maintain ample supply of diapers, wipes, snacks, etc., in the nursery rooms.
- Maintain accurate records of which volunteers served in the nursery rooms during each service.
- Submit any accident reports to parents for signatures and then to the children's ministry administrator after each service.
- Conduct nursery training.
- Serve as "first line of support" to volunteers in the nursery.
- Recruit new volunteers to serve in children's ministry.

Deacon of Community Outreach

This deacon facilitates the involvement of CHBC members in efforts to minister to the local community, publicizes potential ministerial opportunities, and assists the elders in their work to encourage the CHBC membership to evangelize the community.

Duties:

- Coordinate with CHBC staff regarding use of CHBC facilities for evangelistic community outreach efforts, as approved by the elders.
- Assist the elders in encouraging CHBC members to be faithful in caring for the poor and needy in their communities as an outgrowth of their own individual discipleship of Jesus Christ.
- Assist CHBC members in practical ways to become more engaged in serving and caring for needy members of their own communities.
- Serve as a point of first contact for CHBC members seeking advice or assistance to become more engaged in serving and caring for needy persons in their communities.
- Review, evaluate, and maintain relationships with various evangelical organizations ministering to the poor in the D.C. metro area in order to provide information and advice to individual CHBC members seeking to partner with such organizations for volunteer service.

Deacon of Member Care

These deacons have two primary duties: to administer the benevolence fund, and to coordinate ministry to the senior members of the congregation. Additionally, the deacon is occasionally asked to coordinate assistance for members.

The benevolence fund is used to meet the financial needs of the church members, members of the community, or other worthy causes. The fund is administered by the deacon of member care with the oversight of the elders. In order to make a disbursement, the deacon and one elder must agree on the amount and purpose. At that point the church administrator cuts a check from the fund. Disbursements may be accompanied with certain conditions and/or ongoing counseling.

The second primary responsibility of the deacon(s) of member care is to coordinate ministry to the senior members of the congregation. First, the deacon should establish relationships with the senior members in order to better understand and anticipate their needs. Examples of service include coordinating rides to/from church, coordinating rides to/from doctor's appointments, coordinating assistance with yardwork, coordinating Christmas caroling to senior members' homes and other activities.

Deacon of Ordinances

The Deacon of Ordinances is responsible for proper execution of all baptisms and the Lord's Supper.

Duties:

- For baptism, the deacon assists behind the scenes with those involved with the baptism to ensure that things go smoothly and efficiently.
- For the Lord's Supper, the deacon makes sure that the elements are ordered, prepared, and arranged prior to communion; selects members to distribute the Lord's Supper; and assists in the execution of the Supper.

Deacon of Sound

This deacon is responsible for servicing the church's audio projection and recording needs. The deacon should ensure that the sound for all services is clear and non-distracting. He/she should see himself/herself as serving (1) the congregation to minimize distractions from worship; (2) the service leaders and speakers to minimize inconveniences; (3) the world to bring them the recorded Word.

Duties:

- Train volunteers.
- Maintain volunteer schedules and send out reminders as needed.
- Prepare and maintain training and reference materials.
- Periodically retrain volunteers to ensure consistency.
- Manage technical professionals or volunteers to maintain, calibrate, and upgrade sound and recording systems.
- Establish contacts with other churches for ideas on sound ministry.
- Develop methods and standards for audio consistency.
- Come up with a yearly budget for sound system needs.
- Weekly sound quality assurance before Sunday morning service.

Deacon of Ushers

This deacon is responsible for all ushering and greeting during Sunday morning and evening services and at special church functions such as Henry Forums.

Duties:

- Recruiting, scheduling, and managing ushers and greeters, ensuring that they understand their duties and are performing them.
- Managing the offertory and collection. Ensuring offering is collected, consolidated, and stored in safe.
- Being the liaison with the church elders.
- Recommending ways to improve ushering and greeting.

Duties of ushers:

- Greet members and visitors.
- Seat members and visitors.

- Distribute bulletins.
- Ensure efficient use of church seating.
- Answer questions, especially from visitors.
- Assist those needing assistance, especially seniors.
- Ensure accountability in offertory and collection process.
- Ensure proper reverence for God and his Word by discouraging seating and interruptions during prayer and Scripture reading.

Duties of Greeters:

- Greet members and visitors.
- Distribute bulletins.
- Answer questions, especially from visitors.
- Assist those needing assistance, especially seniors.
- Ensure proper reverence for God and his Word by discouraging seating and interruptions during prayer and Scripture reading.

Deacon of Hospitality

This deacon is to provide an environment for visitors/members, believers/non-believers to share refreshments and build relationships through fellowship.

Duties:

- Provide leadership development and oversight for the hospitality ministry.
- Recruit, train, and empower servant leaders in this ministry.
- Help develop talents of others while encouraging them to use their gifts in service.
- Provide ongoing evaluation and development.
- Manage the budget affecting this ministry.

- Inventory control of products, supplies, and equipment necessary to maintain this ministry.
- Liaise with elders.

Functions directly responsible for:

- Sunday Morning West Hall fellowship
- Henry Forum fellowship
- Carols on the Hill
- Member potluck
- Meals to new moms
- Meals to families during sickness/hospital
- Funeral needs
- New members' luncheon

NOTES

1. Louie D. Newton, *Why I Am a Baptist* (Boston: Beacon Press, 1957), 202.

2. For example, Acts 1:17, 25; 19:22; Rom. 12:7; 1 Cor. 12:5; 16:15; Eph. 4:12; Col. 4:17; 2 Tim. 1:18; Philem. 13; Heb. 6:10; 1 Pet. 4:10–11; Rev. 2:19.

3. For example, Rom. 13:4.

4. For example, Matt. 25:44; Acts 11:29; 12:25; Rom. 15:25, 31; 2 Cor. 8:4, 19–20; 9:1, 12–13; 11:8.

5. For example, Matt. 8:15; Mark 1:31; Luke 4:39; Matt. 27:55; Mark 15:41; cp. Luke 8:3; Luke 10:40; John 12:2; Rom. 16:1.

6. For example, Matt. 4:11; Mark 1:13.

7. For example, Matt. 22:13; Luke 10:40; 17:8; John 2:5, 9; 12:2.

8. For example, Matt. 20:28; Mark 10:45; Luke 22:26–27; cp. John 13; Luke 12:37; Romans 15:8.

9. For example, Acts 6:1–7; Acts 20:24; 1 Cor. 3:5; 2 Cor. 3:3, 6–9; 4:1; 5:18; 6:3–4; 11:23; Eph. 3:7; Col. 1:23; 1 Tim. 1:12; 2 Tim. 4:11.

10. Acts 21:19; Rom. 11:13.

11. For example, 1 Tim. 4:6; 2 Tim. 4:5.

12. 1 Pet. 1:12.

13. Heb. 1:14; 2 Cor. 3:6–9; 11:15; Gal. 2:17.

14. Thanks to Pastor Buddy Gray who helped me to see these descriptions.

15. Bonhoeffer, *Life Together: The Classic Exploration of Christian in Community* (New York: Harper & Row, 1954), 109.

16. Os Guinness, *Dining with the Devil* (Grand Rapids, MI: Baker, 1983), 49.

17. For example, see A. T. Robertson, *Life and Letters of John Albert Broadus* (Philadelphia: American Baptist Publication Society, 1902), 34; O. L. Hailey, *The Preaching of J. R. Graves* (1929), 40.

18. See 1 Tim. 5:17; Titus 1:8–9; cp. Acts 6:2, 4.

19. See Timothy Z. Witmer, *The Shepherd Leader: Achieving Effective Shepherding in Your Church* (Phillipsburg, NJ: P&R 2010); also, Phil Newton and Matt Schmucker, *Elders in the Life of the Church* (Wheaton, IL: Crossway, 2014).

20. Jonathan Leeman discusses this matter at length in *Don't Fire Your Church Members: A Case for Congregationalism* (Nashville: B&H Academic,

2016), ch. 5, and at a more popular level in *Understanding the Congregation's Authority* (Nashville: B&H, 2016), ch. 6.

21. Edward Griffin, "A Tearful Farewell from a Faithful Pastor" (1809).

22. Jer. 31:34; 1 Cor. 2:10–16; 1 John 2:20, 27.23. Leeman, *Understanding the Congregation's Authority*, introduction.

SCRIPTURE INDEX